What Would You Do?

By

Kevin Mahaffy, Jr.

What Would You Do?
by Kevin Mahaffy, Jr

Printed in the United States of America

ISBN 978-1-60477-231-9

www.xulonpress.com

Contents

What Would You Do If You Had An Awesome Family?

—⊶⊷—

You would dedicate this book to them!

To my lovely wife Adriana and my two wonderful daughters Claudia and Natalia:

Thanks for your creativity in helping me come up with the questions in this book. I love you beyond words!

What Would You Do If People Helped You With This Book?

—⚬⚬⚬—

You would acknowledge them, of course.

In addition to my family, I would also like to thank Jack Crabtree for his friendship, coaching, constructive feedback, and creative ideas as I learn to write.

Thanks to Pastor Gary Zarlengo and my fellow pastors for encouraging me in youth ministry.

Thanks to my students, fellow youth workers, and friends who have indulged me by allowing me to test out some of these questions on them.

Thanks to my Aunt Susan Spaulding for cleaning up my mess with her editing skills.

Finally, thanks to Mom and Dad, Grandpa and Grandma Mahaffy, and Grandpa and Grandma Larkin. I love you all so much! Thanks for your continued love, support, and encouragement that have made me who I am today and will guide me into the future.

What Would You Do If You Were Asked How You Came Up With This Book?

—∞∞∞—

You would explain it to them.

I was almost thirty-one years old, but the closest I had been to Disneyland or Disney World was the Disney store in the local mall. After a very busy year of ministry, spending virtually every school break with the kids in our youth group, my family needed to get away. Our tax refund was on its way, and we figured we had a small window of opportunity to do something special—a once in a lifetime thing—with our two daughters, then nine and five years old. The girls had been asking us for years to quit trying to trick them into believing that the store in the mall was actually a park and to take them to a real Disney theme park. We decided to visit Disneyland in Anaheim.

Knowing that we would spend a lot of time in lines, we brought some simple things to keep the girls' minds occupied while we inched along. One of those was a new book I had picked up called <u>Choose Your Top 3</u> by Brian Schulenberg.[1] It came in handy almost immediately, as we waited in line to meet the Disney princesses. The book made its way out of my backpack and we began to employ this strategic method of relationship building. Over two hours zipped by while we shared our responses, sometimes seriously, sometimes with peals of laughter.

Throughout our two days in the park we spent time in many long lines and dozens of the top three scenarios listed in the book. At one point a young boy in front of us turned around and offered us his top three. After a few more rounds with the boy fully engaged in the conversation, I asked him where he was from.

"New York," he said.

Surprised, I told him we were from New York as well. "Which part?" I asked.

"Long Island," he responded.

"No way!" I said. "We're from Long Island, too!" It turns out we lived only twenty minutes apart. I gave his dad my card and invited the boy to come out and visit our youth ministry. How neat that a simple conversation starter like *Choose Your Top 3* had perked a stranger's interest and prompted him to jump into a conversation which led to a potentially meaningful connection!

I am not sure if it was the California sun beating down on my head or what, but at some point in some long line in Disneyland, a scene from *Napoleon Dynamite* popped into my mind.

Don: "Hey Napoleon, what did you do all last summer again?"

Napoleon Dynamite: "I told you. I spent it with my uncle in Alaska hunting wolverines."

Don: "Did you shoot any?"

Napoleon Dynamite: "Yes, like 50 of 'em! They kept trying to attack my cousins. What the heck would you do in a situation like that?"[2]

We all laughed as I quoted the scene to my wife and kids. Then I said, "Hey, what if we came up with our own list of 'What the heck would you do in a situation like that' questions?" Over the next week we brainstormed questions about everything we could imagine.

And that's how this book was birthed.

What Would You Do If You Were Asked How To Use This Book?

———∞∞∞———

You would read below.

This book includes a wide range of questions for teens. Some are funny; others are serious. Some are shallow; others are deep. Some deal with kids' emotions; others deal with their spirituality. Some deal with ethics while others deal with relationships. Some will elicit humorous responses, but others will get people thinking. Some will bring about surface answers, while others will reach deep into teens' hearts and minds and prompt revelation of their beliefs, values, motives, hurts, fears, joys, and more. They are in no particular order, and even though a question might say "him" or "her," just about every question can apply to guys or girls. The stories that are told throughout the book are true, but real names have been changed to protect the innocent. (I've always wanted to say that!)

Use wisdom when selecting which questions to use in your given context. For instance, if someone in your group has bad body odor, you wouldn't want to use question #142! Know your audience and be sensitive to their situations.

Release your creativity in how and when to use the questions. I have used these questions as time-killers on road trips, as icebreakers in small groups, as crowd-mixers in large groups, and in one-on-one conversations. Invite teens to act out, write, or draw their responses, not just voice them. The possibilities are endless!

Remember the goal. The questions are simply non-threatening tools to get people talking. If someone doesn't speak another word for the remainder of your time together, he or she will have said something in response to at least one question. Beyond getting them to talk, their responses will also give you glimpses into teens' lives and thought patterns.

Below are some *practical ideas to get the most out of your question and answer time.*

- Don't settle for yes/no or Sunday school answers. (The questions are not designed for yes/no answers, but kids have an amazing ability to try them anyhow.) Try to get into their thought processes. If you receive a yes/no or "I dunno" shrug, dig deeper: Why did you respond with the answer you did? If you have really been through a similar situation, how did it make you feel? What emotions did you experience?

- Ask if a response is theoretical (the answer someone *thinks* you are looking for) or if thoughtful and truthful (how that person would actually respond in a given situation). For example, question 9 reads, *What would you do if you saw a new kid being ignored at youth group?* Someone feeling guilty for having done just that the week before might respond that she would sit with that person and get to know her. Probe gently: Are you saying that just because it *seems* like the right answer? You could then capitalize on a teachable moment and open the door to meaningful discussion.

- Be ready to rephrase the question. If your kids misunderstand a question, get side-tracked on loopholes, or otherwise begin to stray from the point, repackage the question in a way that leads to clearer focus.

- Be ready to ask another question if one doesn't work. If, despite your efforts, your kids don't understand a question or are simply unresponsive, pull out another one and give it a try. Don't get discouraged. Don't take it personally. Just move on.

- Be sure to communicate that there are no right or wrong answers. As you discuss a question, you might help your teens discover if their responses are consistent with who they are and what they claim to believe. Be sure that you foster an atmosphere in which they feel safe to think out loud and express themselves without the fear of others judging them for their vulnerability and authenticity.

- Be sure that everyone participates. Don't let Johnny answer all of the questions or cut off those who are trying to think of and share their responses. When one person dominates the talking, others will either get frustrated or they will feel relieved that they don't have to talk because they have Johnny as their spokesperson. Neither is helpful to the communication process or your connection as a group.

What Would You Do **Questions**

—⚇—

1. If you were going to lose all but two of your memories?

2. If you could only listen to one song on your iPod before it would self-destruct?

3. If Instant Messaging ended?

4. If you could only get one possession (not a person or pet) out of your house before it burned to the ground?

5. If your mom and dad said you could choose any place in the world to go on a family vacation?

6. If you lost your passport while on a missions trip in a Third World country?

7. If your parents disapproved of the person you wanted to date?

8. If you could tell your senior pastor to change one thing about your church?

9. If you saw a new kid being ignored at youth group?

10. If you had to wear skirts for the rest of your life?

11. If you found a wallet with one thousand dollars in it but no identification?

12. If you noticed that the cashier put one of your items into the bag without charging you for it?

13. If someone pushed you into a pool?

14. If you found out that you were done growing and were as tall as you're going to get?

15. If you ran into someone you had been trying to avoid?

16. If your swimming suit fell off while water skiing?

17. If you were at home alone late at night and you heard someone trying to break in?

18. If you could change one thing about Starbucks?

19. If you found a lamp, rubbed it, a genie came out and said he would grant you one wish?

20. If you had the opportunity to ask your parents one question without feeling embarrassed?

21. If your mom and dad said it was OK for you to get a tattoo?

22. If God asked you to write a book of the Bible?

23. If you were stranded in the middle of the desert?

24. If you were guaranteed success?

25. If you were asked by your youth pastor to spend your youth group's budget?

26. If you were asked to come up with one solution for ending world hunger?

27. If you could build your dream house?

28. If your parents said you could move to another state?

29. If the pilot of your plane came on the loudspeaker and said your plane was going down?

30. If you felt that you were about to rip one in the church van—and your senior pastor was driving?

31. If you could spend the day with Jesus?

32. If you knew that your best friend was going to a party that his parents had explicitly forbidden him/her to attend?

33. If you slipped and fell in the mud in front of the guy or girl that you were about to ask out?

34. If your brother or sister had the remote control and your parents said you had to watch whatever he or she wanted?

35. If you were mistakenly identified as a suspect in a police lineup?

36. If you were singing a solo at church and forgot the lyrics?

37. If McDonald's went out of business?

38. If it became illegal to be a Christian?

39. If your favorite pet died?

40. If a longtime friend told you he or she was gay?

41. If your boyfriend/girlfriend said no when you asked him or her to marry you?

42. If you found out that you had one year to live?

43. If there were no cell phones?

44. If you could spend the day with the President of the United States?

45. If you made it onto your favorite reality show?

46. If you won on your favorite reality show?

47. If you overflowed the toilet at the home of your prom date, the bathroom had no plunger, and the entire family was waiting for you outside the door?

48. If you could design your own home with "Extreme Makeover: Home Edition"?

49. If you won a drawing for your favorite band to play a private party for you and ten of your closest friends?

50. If you found pornographic websites listed in the history of your friend's computer?

51. If you started going bald at age twenty-one?

52. If you saw your best friend with a booger hanging out of his nose while you were both with a group of friends?

53. If you could do one more thing before going completely blind?

54. If you saw your dad getting a pedicure?

55. If you spilled lemonade on your lap while wearing white pants?

56. If you found out that you missed the Rapture?

57. If you could only choose one way to grow in your relationship with Jesus?

58. If there was no Internet?

59. If you had unlimited strength?

60. If you could add one thing to your youth group that would help attract unchurched kids?

61. If you could fly?

62. If it rained on the day of your planned outdoor wedding and you did not have a backup location?

63. If you could see God's heart for a person you currently have a conflict with?

64. If you could undo one thing from your past?

65. If you could travel back to any point in history to visit for a week?

66. If you showed up at the airport and were told that the nonrefundable ticket you had purchased was for another day?

67. If you could see the effects of the choices you make today and their impact on your life twenty years from now?

68. If you and your friends got together to play board games all night?

69. If you found out you were having quadruplets?

70. If your friend asked you how being a Christ-follower was different from being a Buddhist?

71. If you could tell your brother or sister one thing before you knew you would never see him or her again?

72. If you could eliminate one rule that your parents have for you and replace it with another one?

73. If you felt like your parents favored your sibling(s) over you?

74. If you could do one kind thing for a stranger today?

75. To encourage a friend who is going through a tough time this week?

76. If you were suddenly transported to a totally new place and had to make friends?

77. If someone enlisted you in the military, and you couldn't convince the military that you hadn't signed up?

78. If your tent and all of your belongings got completely swamped during a thunderstorm while you were camping?

79. If you found out your youth pastor or youth leaders wanted to quit because they felt like they were not making a difference?

80. If you were at the zoo and an announcement came over the loudspeaker that a tiger had escaped?

81. If you were on the Titanic when it started to sink?

82. If you could spend the day with one person from the Old Testament?

83. If, like, fifty wolverines were attacking your cousins? (See "What Would You Do If You Were Asked How You Came Up With This Book?")

84. If you were in a car accident and instantly became a quadriplegic?

85. If a known killer broke into your house, put a gun to your head, and demanded to know if anyone else was in the house — and your children were hiding in a closet?

86. If a Jewish person asked you to show him how you believe Jesus fulfilled Messianic prophecies?

87. If you could change one law?

88. If you were offered the leading role in a major Hollywood movie but would have to do something that violated your convictions?

89. If you saw someone being beaten up and robbed by a group of thugs, but you were all by yourself?

90. If you had one more hour each day?

91. If you could add one word to the English language?

92. If you saw someone shoplifting?

93. If you saw a rat running around the kitchen in your favorite restaurant?

94. If mullets were back in style?

95. If you were carrying leftovers from your favorite restaurant and saw a homeless person looking for dinner in the garbage?

96. If you were stuck in the airport all day?

97. If you waited for three hours to ride your favorite roller coaster and when you finally got to the front of the line they announced that it had broken down and would be out of commission for the rest of the day?

98. If you were walking down the aisle at your wedding when you suddenly felt a violent pain and knew that you had diarrhea?

99. If you could bring one person back to life?

Billy's Story

When his mom came to me and informed me that 16-year-old Billy (not his real name) was struggling in school, I decided to take him out for pizza. Since he was fairly new to our youth ministry, I wanted to spend some time getting to know him before addressing his academic issues.

Billy and I laughed our way through several simple, humorous questions before I asked, "What would you do if you could bring one person back to life?" He didn't hesitate. "My dad, of course," he said.

Billy had lost his dad to a sudden heart attack the previous year. What was your dad like? I asked. What did you most admire about your dad? What is your favorite memory of him? How did he respond when you were going through a tough time? How do you handle tough times now without him around?

These follow-up questions allowed Billy to revisit cherished memories of his dad. They also opened the door for us to engage in a discussion about the problem at hand. After Billy shared his memories of his dad, I asked him if he was presently struggling with anything in particular. He opened up to me about his difficulties in school and shared that he had basically given up and resigned himself to failing his classes. What would your dad want you to do, I asked. Billy admitted that his dad would want him to keep trying. I was able to encourage him to move forward, and do his best to dig himself out of his academic hole. I then prayed for Billy.

On the ride home I thanked Billy for the opportunity to spend some time with him. I told him that I appreciated his openness in sharing with me about his father. I'd be checking up on him, I told Billy, and let him know that if he ever needed a man to talk to, our male adult youth leaders and I would be there for him.

About a week later I received this e-mail from Billy's mom:

Dear Pastor Kevin,

You just don't know how happy I was to hear that Billy spoke to you about his father. As you know, I have been very concerned about my son for quite awhile. I believed that much of the troubles stemmed from his inability to grieve or talk about his father. Hearing that he spoke about his father and did not change the subject is, as I see it, a step in the right direction. Thank you, Pastor Kevin.

Sincerely,
Billy's Mom

Questions are a tremendous tool that God can use to open the door to transformational conversations. Next time you read the Gospels, note how often Jesus used questions in His interactions with people. He showed us how questions can be a powerful instrument in the hands of those who are committed to meaningful, life-changing conversations.

100. If you were given two front row seats to a Broadway play?

101. If someone told you he was going to commit suicide but asked you not to tell anyone?

102. If you discovered that someone had stolen your identity and was living as *you* in another country?

103. If your friends started teasing someone in front of you?

104. If there was no MySpace?

105. If Bill Gates asked you to take over Microsoft?

106. If someone asked you how being a Christ-follower differed from being a Muslim?

107. If you were playing a pick-up game of basketball and noticed that two players were about to fight each other?

108. If you had to wear skintight leather pants for the rest of your life?

109. If you could write a book about something of great interest to you?

110. For a dollar—right now?

111. If your friends were trying to get you to pull a joke on someone so they could all have a good laugh, but you knew that the joke would hurt the person's feelings and/or embarrass her?

112. If you found a pornographic magazine on the way home from school but no one saw you find it?

113. If you went to the ATM after hours to withdrawal money from your bank account that you knew had five thousand dollars in it, then received a message that you had a zero balance?

114. If you were given a chance to direct a hit Hollywood movie?

115. If an angel appeared to you?

116. If you walked in on some of your friends doing drugs?

117. If the only job you could get was at Burger King?

118. If you were at home during a thunder-storm watching a scary movie when suddenly the power went out and you heard a knock at the door?

119. If you woke up on prom day with three big zits on your face?

120. If you were out of paint and hiding during a game of paintball when you realized that you were lying in poison ivy, but the opposing team was walking all around you?

121. If you found out your every move was being watched like what happened in the movie "The Truman Show"?

122. If God said you could be in charge of the world for a week?

123. If people could read your thoughts on a screen on your forehead?

124. If you could change one thing about your favorite fast food restaurant?

125. If you were trapped in your room for an entire week?

126. If you were in a public restroom and discovered, after going number two, that your stall had no toilet paper?

127. If your boss told you that due to financial problems he would not be able to pay you for your past two weeks of work?

128. If you couldn't watch your favorite show and asked your mom to record it for you, but when you got home you discovered that the tape was blank?

129. If God asked you not to engage in any romantic relationships until you had completed your college degree?

130. If you found out that your family was in serious debt?

131. If you arrived at your destination after flying all day and discovered that your luggage had mistakenly been sent somewhere else?

132. If your cell phone died during the middle of a 9-1-1 call?

133. If you discovered that someone had hacked into your e-mail account and read all of your messages?

134. If someone signed you up for a talent show?

135. If you found out that your parents were not your biological parents but had actually adopted you as an infant?

136. If you were going through security at the airport, the airplane door was about to close, and security said that all the gifts in your carry-on that you had purchased while on vacation either had to be thrown away or you would have to go back and check them and miss your flight?

137. If you were in a theater and noticed the person in front of you videotaping the movie?

138. If the elderly lady sitting next to you on the plane urinated in her seat but didn't seem to notice right before you departed on a five-hour flight?

139. If someone crashed into your house with his car?

140. If you ran into someone in the mall who looked just like you and discovered that you were twins separated at birth?

141. If you won a $10,000 shopping spree at the mall?

142. If a friend had really bad body odor?

143. If you were forced to eat Taco Bell food at every meal for the rest of your life?

144. If you were on a missions trip and the only food available to you was monkey brains?

145. If you became a teenager at the same time your parents were teenagers and you all attended the same school?

146. If the governor came to your house for dinner?

147. If you were selected by NASA to go to the moon?

148. If "SpongeBob SquarePants" was canceled?

149. If you had no hands?

150. If you were the sole survivor of an accident which claimed the lives of your entire family?

151. If you locked yourself out of your house and no one else was home?

152. If you were asked which emotion is the hardest for you to experience?

153. If you were the king of a small country?

154. If while hiking you came face to face with a grizzly bear?

155. If you found a used Band-Aid in the burger you were eating?

156. If you knew that God wouldn't forgive you because you refused to forgive other people?

157. If your parents told you that you could no longer have a MySpace account?

158. If you looked out the window of the plane, saw an engine on fire, and reported it to the pilot—but he didn't believe you?

159. If your friend said that truth is whatever each person decides it is?

160. If your boyfriend/girlfriend of two years said that if you really loved him/her you would have sex with him/her?

161. If you came home from school and found a ransom note demanding money or you would never see your favorite pet again?

162. If you were offered your inheritance now or in ten years?

163. If you discovered that you had contracted AIDS after being accidentally scratched with a dirty needle?

164. If Apple put Microsoft out of business?

165. If you got up in the middle of the night and in the dark stepped on a dog dropping with your bare feet?

166. If you discovered that someone was spying on you?

167. If someone stole your computer?

168. If heavy metal was the only kind of music?

169. If Google didn't exist?

170. If you were in the mall and found a pair of pants you really wanted but were five dollars short, but you had your parents' credit card which they said you could only use for food?

171. If you were flying standby with your entire family and only one seat was available on the next flight?

172. If you had to choose to be deaf or mute?

173. If you had your purse or wallet stolen while in a theme park and saw someone in line to buy something holding one that looked just like yours?

174. If you were the only person in the room when a very ill family member passed away?

175. If you were offered one complimentary steak dinner at Outback Steakhouse OR free hamburgers for you and three friends for a week at Wendy's?

176. If while riding the subway you felt someone trying to pick your pocket?

177. If you had to wear baggy clothes for the rest of your life?

178. If doctors told you that you had a rare disease and your face would be completely covered with hair like a werewolf for the rest of your life?

179. If you found out that your mom or dad was a gambling addict and had gambled away your college savings?

180. If your boat capsized in the middle of the Atlantic Ocean and you saw only one life jacket in the water—you knew how to swim, but you saw someone just a few feet away who obviously didn't?

181. If you could do something to convince Barbara Walters to name you one of the most fascinating people of the year?

182. If you fell asleep on the beach without sunblock and woke up to find that you were completely sunburned except for the word "dork" which your friends had written on your forehead with sunblock as you slept?

183. If you had to go to school all year round?

184. If you were accepted to your favorite college but would have to pay your own way or were offered a full scholarship to the arch-rival college?

185. If you arrived at the bank to cash your paycheck the day before a holiday weekend and they had just locked the door?

186. If winter lasted ten months a year?

187. If you could choose any place in the world to live?

188. If the airline would not allow you to board the plane because several people had complained about your body odor?

189. If your last name rhymed with an embarrassing word?

190. If your prom date stood you up?

191. If you came down with malaria?

192. If your parents told you they were getting a divorce?

193. If you were given four front row seats to your favorite sporting event?

194. If you were stuck in a car for twelve hours and the driver was cranking country music?

195. If a waiter spilled her entire tray of food and drinks on your lap?

196. If you could change any part of your name?

197. If your parents told you they had arranged a marriage for you?

198. If you were on a missions trip in a Third World country and one of the people on your team started experiencing a stroke?

199. If you could rewrite "Old MacDonald Had a Farm" with lyrics about the person to your left?

Old MacSometimes!

Question #199 is one of those questions that works great sometimes while at other times it flops. The first time I tried this question on a group of teens was during a student leadership retreat. Before resuming our teaching session, I posed this question to them. After a few embarrassing moments of staring at one another, they embraced the challenge. For the next ten minutes the room was filled with hysterical laughter as they fumbled through their creative rhymes. What a great experience!

The next weekend I worked with a different bunch of students. I anticipated a similar response to that of my student leaders just days earlier. Instead, they gave me those blank stares that every youth leader *loves* to see (not!) when he thinks he has given his students something fun to do. I pressed them to give it a try, but they wouldn't budge. They asked me to sing the song about someone. I did, but they dug their heels in and refused to give it a shot.

A few days later I tried the question with a third group, again with success. Why didn't it work all three times? I had to remind myself that kids don't respond identically to each question. Sometimes it depends on the group, and other times it depends upon the occasion. Keep in mind that kids are riding an emotional roller coaster during their teenage years. You might have them fully engaged one week and totally disengaged the next. You might not have changed. Your question might not have changed. But in that short a time your students will have changed. Don't get discouraged. Don't take it personally. Just move on and ask them another question.

200. If someone offered you $5 to wear a clean diaper on your head around school for an entire day?

201. If you observed the quarterback of the football team cheating on a test the week before the state championship game, and you knew that your team couldn't win without him?

202. If you saw a kid you disliked cheating on a test?

203. If you could start a new hobby?

204. If you could overcome one fear that you have?

205. If you came outside and found that your car had been stolen?

206. If your teacher told you that you could give yourself your final grade, but you had skipped 75% of the classes?

207. If you could have a conversation with an atheist?

208. If Coke put Pepsi out of business?

209. If you found out that your neighbor was the antichrist?

210. If you entered a sporting event and by total coincidence they seated you right next to your hero?

211. If your birthday was on Christmas day, but you didn't get more or better presents than anyone else?

212. If you got lost in the woods while on a camping trip?

213. If your friends started making fun of or gossiping about someone who wasn't there?

214. If the Yankees moved to Boston, and the Red Sox moved to New York?

215. If you were suddenly homeless?

216. If you went to hear your favorite band in concert, but when you got there they had been replaced by another band?

217. If you found dead flies in the bottom of your soup?

218. If you could ask God to clarify something from the Bible that confuses you?

219. If ice cream was proven to cause cancer?

220. If you overslept and missed your exams?

221. If you saw that someone who you respect was on TV being arrested?

222. If the person you are having the greatest problem with right now never changed?

223. If you had unlimited resources and could do anything you wanted?

224. If the roller coaster in which you were riding malfunctioned, leaving you suspended upside down?

225. If you were a baseball fan sitting along the left field line, your team was one out away from going to the World Series, and you reached out and caught a foul ball that could have been caught by the outfielder on your team to end the game AND your team went on to lose the game?

226. If you owned your own island?

227. If you were offered one thousand dollars to let Mike Tyson hit you in the head just one time?

228. If you were Job from the Bible?

229. If you got lost in a country and did not speak the language?

230. If you slipped and fell off a cruise ship?

231. If your doctor put an X-ray on the screen after your surgery and you noticed that he had left a pair of scissors inside of you?

232. If the person sitting next to you on the plane started snoring loudly?

233. If your computer crashed when you were writing the final sentence of your twenty-five page term paper and you hadn't backed it up?

234. If you were having suicidal thoughts?

235. If your wedding photographer called you and told you that he had accidentally permanently deleted all of your wedding photos?

236. If someone you loved was serving time in prison?

237. If you lost your wedding ring?

238. If you got stuck in an elevator in the Sears Tower in Chicago?

239. If you were Joseph and your fiancée Mary came in and told you she was pregnant—by God?

240. If someone asked you why it is important for Christ-followers to be water baptized?

241. If you had to wear a suit every day?

242. If you held a record which was broken by someone who was suspected of cheating?

243. If the person sitting next to you on the plane pulled out a pornographic magazine?

244. If you were a real jerk to someone because you thought they were lying to you about something but later found out that they had been telling you the truth?

245. If you were the police chief in your city?

246. If you had to eliminate one of your five senses?

247. If you were asked which of your emotions is the hardest for you to hide?

248. If you had to stand up in front of people and talk for forty-five minutes?

249. If you saw yourself on the big screen at a sporting event?

250. If your mom washed your favorite tee shirt and it came out pink?

251. If someone else was given the leading role in your school's play because he was the teacher's favorite student even though you had clearly outperformed him during auditions?

252. If the school bully said he would be waiting in the parking lot after school to beat you up?

253. If you heard a rumor that two boys were planning to bring guns to school?

254. If you sent someone a package for Christmas and it got lost in the mail?

255. If your luggage did not make it to your destination while traveling, your suitcases were delivered to you two days later, and you discovered that the locks had been cut off and someone had stolen some items?

256. If you accidentally broke the vase containing your grandma's ashes?

257. If you could tell your youth pastor to change one thing about your youth group?

258. If the deer in the back of your truck, which you thought you had killed while hunting, suddenly jumped up and started thrashing around while you were driving home?

259. If you wanted to make the person next to you laugh right now?

260. If you were told that you had failed your senior year of high school and would have to repeat it?

261. If you were lost in the Amazon and came upon a cannibalistic tribe?

262. If your dad's hobby was collecting rattlesnakes?

263. If someone in your circle of friends was making racial jokes?

264. If you could take back something that you said to someone?

265. If you ran your own company?

266. If your friend said she believed Jesus was a good person but wasn't God?

267. If you found out that your father was a secret agent for the government?

268. If you were a soldier sent to fight in a war that you disagreed with?

269. If you married someone from another country, but after visiting relatives in his/her homeland your government would not allow him/her to reenter your country?

270. If you found out your mom or dad was a closet alcoholic?

271. If you were on the cover of a tabloid?

272. If you had just finished building your dream house and a hurricane came through and destroyed it a week after you moved in?

273. If you were asked why it is important to be a part of a local church?

274. If someone demanded you to walk on broken glass with bare feet or they would

broadcast your secret sins over the loud-speaker at school?

275. If you found out that you had been dropped from someone's list of top friends on MySpace?

276. If you could name a dog or cat?

277. If you were offered ten million dollars by the world's best tightrope walker to get on his back as he walked across a tightrope over Niagara Falls?

278. If you could choose one friend to be your partner on "The Amazing Race"?

279. If your friend wanted you to drive her to get an abortion so her parents wouldn't find out that she was pregnant?

280. If rap was the only kind of music?

281. If you could make the announcements on an airplane?

282. If there were no such thing as video games?

283. If you could create a new flavor of ice cream?

284. If a friend invited you to run with the bulls in Pamplona, Spain?

285. If you found out that the underwear you bought was marked down because it had been returned to the store—*used*?

286. If the pilot of your plane came on over the loudspeaker and said that the wheels were stuck and he was going to have to land the plane on its belly?

287. If you were a slave in the United States before the Civil War?

288. If someone shaved your head while you were sleeping?

289. If your best friend started dating your ex-boyfriend/ex-girlfriend?

290. If you got amnesia and woke up in a city not knowing who you were, where you were, or what you were doing there?

291. If you broke wind in an elevator filled with people?

292. If you had to sing a song for karaoke night?

293. If the President invited you to work in the White House?

294. If you saw your best friend on "America's Most Wanted"?

295. If you knew when Jesus was going to return?

296. If you saw a thief in the mall being chased by police and he was running right toward you?

297. If your parents wanted you to become a lawyer, but you felt that God wanted you to be a pastor?

298. If you knew that the school bully was about to leave school and get into a fatal car accident?

299. If you were driving down a mountain and your brakes went out?

Do You Really Believe in the Power of Prayer?

It was the first missions trip experience for nearly every one of the twenty-five student on our team. We had fled the chill of New York for the warmth of Georgia to serve Jesus! So far everything had been going great. All of their hard work learning songs, dances, dramas, and how to share their testimonies was paying off. They had successfully led a Sunday morning service at the church with which we were working, and the mayor of Toccoa, Georgia had even presented them with a plaque for their service in the community. The kids were flying high!

During every missions trip it's important to have a day of fun where the team can explore the area, and this trip was no exception. After breakfast about halfway through the trip we headed out for our day of downtime. The first thing we did was descend the Tallulah Gorge. But after enjoying the view from the bottom for a while, we had to climb back up the thousand or so feet we had just come down. When we arrived at the top most of the team collapsed on the ground in exhaustion. So much for relaxation!

After lunch we loaded into our three vehicles and began to drive through the Smoky Mountains on our way Gatlinburg, Tennessee. The drive was over thirty miles of winding up, down, and around the mountains. We had driven more than halfway through mountains, with the students in my van singing songs, telling stories, and laughing in the back as I drove. As we wound our way down the side of one mountain I pressed my foot against the brake.

The vehicle didn't slow down.

I navigated around the next turn and tried again. Nothing! My brakes were gone! The singing tapered off, and smiling faces went pale. Tersely I asked everyone if they really believed in the power of prayer. If they did, it was time to put that belief into practice! I asked them to pray for God to give me wisdom and to protect us in the midst of this scary and dangerous situation. One by one the wan faces regained color as they lifted their voices to the Lord, asking Him to give me wisdom and to protect us in this scary and dangerous situation.

We continued to cruise down the mountain until I found a section of road that wasn't as steep as others. I decided to give the emergency brake a shot. After breathing a quick prayer myself, I pulled it. It wasn't pretty, but I got the vehicle stopped safely.

We allowed the vehicle to rest as the brakes cooled down. After consulting with the other leaders, we decided to sandwich my vehicle between the other two and drive the remainder of the way through the mountains into Gatlinburg, TN.

We arrived in Gatlinburg, TN just after 6 p.m. All the repair shops were closed. While the team goofed off together, a few of the leaders and I deliberated over our options during dinner. We chose to skip the mountains and return to Toccoa via the less up-and-down highway. The brakes cooled down substantially and worked fine for the rest of our trip.

The next day the whole team met to talk about the previous day's adventure. Valuable life lessons that went well beyond vehicles were discussed. Our escapade with the van provided a valuable faith-builder for the moldable young minds that rode with me that day in the Smoky Mountains.

300. If you looked like a celebrity?

301. If you found out that your hotel bed was infested with lice?

302. If you left your little brother/sister in the mall and didn't realize it until you were on your way home?

303. If you could learn any musical instrument?

304. If short gym shorts came back into style for guys?

305. If your family forgot your birthday?

306. If your best friend said that he/she was moving across country in two weeks?

307. If people made fun of you because you were different?

308. If you were attacked by a rabid raccoon?

309. If you didn't like your roommate at college?

310. If you had the opportunity to purchase a sports team?

311. If you could do something about Donald Trump's hair?

312. If chocolate could no longer be manufactured?

313. If you could select one clothing style for everyone in the world?

314. If you were bleeding after your boat capsized in shark-infested waters?

315. If your cat ate your bird?

316. If there was a 9 p.m. curfew for teen-agers in your town during the summer?

317. If you were asked to write a new "Lord of the Rings" movie?

318. If your kidney was a perfect match for someone who needed a transplant?

319. If you could tell your parents today one thing you appreciate about them?

320. If a scientist offered to clone you?

321. If you discovered that aliens were real and your neighbor was one?

322. If your friends were all getting tattoos on spring break but your parents had told you specifically not to get one?

323. If you had one hundred dollars right now?

324. If you could choose a restaurant to take everyone to tonight?

325. If you were wearing clothes at school which you thought were clean, but they were actually dirty and had accidentally been folded and put into your drawer— and they started to smell?

326. If you saw someone with his zipper down?

327. If you could relive one moment from the previous week?

328. If you could undo one thing from the previous week?

329. If someone's dog ran out in front of your car while you were driving and you hit it?

330. If you were told that you would be killed if you chose to follow Christ?

331. If girls couldn't wear makeup?

332. If there were no cars?

333. If you were depressed?

334. If your mom or dad decided to go to college with you?

335. If you found out a friend was anorexic or bulimic?

336. If you went on whale watch but didn't see any whales?

337. If someone was rubbing her finger-nails down a chalkboard demanding the combination to your locker?

338. If you accidentally threw away your parents' income tax return check?

339. If you were in the middle of the forest, your arm was trapped under a log for two days with no real prospect of anyone finding you, and you had a pocket knife?

340. If someone you had significantly invested your life in decided to walk away from everything she knew to be right and true?

341. If you were asked to explain why it bothered you that the person in the previous question would walk away from what he knew to be right and true?

342. If you were kicked out of an all-you-can-eat buffet for eating too much?

343. If you served 25 years in prison for a crime you didn't commit before DNA evidence cleared you?

344. If you were a soldier at the crucifixion of Jesus?

345. If your child was kidnapped?

346. If you were asked to kill one person in order to save a million people?

347. If you saw trash on the floor in the youth room?

348. If you discovered that your house was built on a landfill filled with hazardous waste?

349. If you could tell us who Jesus is to you and how He influences your life on a daily basis?

350. If you could invent something that would change the way people live?

351. If you had to wear high heels every day for the rest of your life?

352. If you could tell a little white lie and avoid a detention?

353. If you ran out of gas in the middle of the highway during rush hour?

354. If your friend asked you if you believed in a literal hell and if you thought that a loving God would actually send people there?

355. If you bit into a piece of fruit and it was full of maggots?

356. If you had to walk five miles to school every day?

357. If your dad was colorblind and accidentally wore your mom's pink socks to church?

358. If you successfully snuck out of the house, but when you returned at 4 a.m. your dad was sitting in the darkened kitchen and said, "Busted!" when you walked in?

359. If you overheard three men in the mall talking about a bank robbery?

360. If you were at security in the airport and realized that after a recent hunting trip you had forgotten to take a large knife out of the side pocket of the backpack you were now carrying?

361. If soap operas ended?

362. If your birthday was February 29th?

363. If you were facing bankruptcy?

364. If your friend asked why he should be a Christ-follower?

365. If your fiancé (or fiancée) didn't show up for your wedding?

366. If you were asked to create a new video game?

367. If you were brought back to life after seeing heaven?

368. If you were in a hurry to get somewhere but had locked your keys in the car?

369. If a friend told you she regularly cut herself?

370. If you could change one thing about the healthcare system?

371. If you found out your dad was a hit man in the Mafia?

372. If your child told you he thought he might be gay?

373. If you could be fluent in another language?

374. If you were asked to carry the cross for Jesus on His way to Calvary?

375. If you were asked if Mormons would go to heaven?

376. If God asked you to fast from food for one month?

377. If someone told you a sickness or pain you were experiencing was proof of sin in your life?

378. If you found out that your friend was talking about you behind your back?

379. If there were no Wal-Marts?

380. If you were a new kid at youth group and no one made any effort to reach out or get to know you?

381. If you lost an envelope that contained your house key and home address while in the grocery store?

382. If you suffered third-degree burns over 90% of your body?

383. If you struck out in slow pitch softball?

384. If you were asked to develop a new flavor of Slurpee?

385. If you worked for the Department of Motor Vehicles?

386. If you found out that your dad had spent time in jail for robbery before you were born?

387. If you had to explain yourself using coffee terms?

388. If you were in charge of your youth group's worship team and someone auditioned to sing or play an instrument but he wasn't very good?

389. If you found out that you would grow to be over seven feet tall?

390. If someone posted your address and home phone number on MySpace?

391. If you could live in a house for free but you were not able to move any of the furniture or redecorate?

392. If your doctor told you that your voice was forever stuck in the state of puberty?

393. If you wrote a play for drama class and five years later saw your teacher had produced it as a movie?

394. If you discovered that a TV show was based on your family?

395. If you were invited to climb Mt. Everest?

396. If you had a hairy back?

397. If you could travel the world for one month?

398. If a dog urinated on your leg?

399. If you were asked to explain the difference between Christianity and Catholicism?

John's Girlfriend

John (not his real name) and I were enjoying some Starbucks Frappucinos as we walked through the park. "Do you have a girlfriend?" I asked.

"Yes," said John.

I encouraged John to tell me about her. She was a nice girl from school. They had been going out for a few months. When I inquired about where she was at on her spiritual journey, John informed me that she was Catholic. He had been bringing her to youth group for some time. I asked him what she thought of our youth group. He said she enjoyed it, but they had never really talked about their beliefs.

I then asked John, "What would you do if she asked you the difference(s) between Christianity and Catholicism?"

"I'm really not sure," he said.

I asked if he could identify some potential differences between the two.

"They pray to the saints and we don't," he said.

"Why do they pray to the saints, and why do we not pray to the saints?" I followed up.

"Why would you pray to the saints when you can pray directly to God?" He wondered.

"What other differences can you think of?"

"They believe in Purgatory."

"What is Purgatory?" I asked.

"It's where people go when they die, I think."

"Let's push your relationship ahead a few years," I said. I painted a picture where she stayed Catholic, he remained a Christian, and invited him to imagine that in five years they decided to get married. I asked him to consider some questions such as:

• What church will you get married in?
• Who will perform your wedding?
• Do you know what the Catholic church's stance would be on your religion?
• What would they have to say about the religion you will raise your children in?
• What about when your children are born?
• What is one of the first things your Catholic wife would want to do with your children?
• What is your understanding of baptism?

At age sixteen these questions seem too unimportant to bring up with his girlfriend. But left unanswered these questions could lead to a major crisis of faith and conflict if their relationship progressed.

I challenged John to prayerfully consider the differences between Catholicism and Christianity. Many Catholics have a genuine relationship with

God through Jesus Christ. I in no way intend to discredit their faith, but even a quick examination will reveal significant theological differences between the two. I didn't answer the questions that I threw at John that day. My aim was to get him using the mind that the Lord gave him. I encouraged John to begin a dialogue about these issues with his parents and with his girlfriend.

400. If you were sent to live with your grand-parents for the summer?

401. If you unloaded your car after grocery shopping on Friday but accidentally left fresh fish in the back seat and didn't discover it until Sunday morning when you were about to leave for church?

402. If you were a fashion model and tripped on the runway during a show?

403. If you could cancel one television show?

404. If you felt like your parents were trying to live their own dreams out through you?

405. If you were elected President of the United States?

406. If you had a baby at the age of 65?

407. If one of your unmarried friends told you that she was pregnant?

408. If someone asked you what qualities she should look for in a local church?

409. If you saw your cat being squeezed by a python?

410. If you were riding a horse that refused to obey your commands?

411. If someone said he was worried that he had committed the unpardonable sin (Matthew 12:31-32) because he had recorded himself saying that he denied the existence of the Holy Spirit and had posted it on YouTube?

412. If you went on a youth trip and had to room with people you didn't know?

413. If you could come up with one way to serve your community this month?

414. If the government reinstituted the military draft?

415. If prayer was legally allowed back into public schools?

416. If you were asked to create a wrestling character?

417. If your grandmother gave you an ugly sweater for Christmas and expected you to wear it to church the next day?

418. If you were asked to create a new board game?

419. If you went undefeated all season but lost the championship game?

420. If someone was serving a life sentence for committing a serious crime against you and you were asked to forgive him?

421. If the police busted you while you were pulling a prank?

422. If you were asked to describe what you would consider a perfect local church?

423. If you were asked to be in your friend's wedding but you didn't feel good about the person she was marrying?

424. If someone gave you a present that you didn't want, and you planned to attend friend's party in a week and needed a present for him?

425. If you were swimming in the ocean and the lifeguard yelled, "Shark!"?

426. If your teacher was mocking someone in your class for not embracing the theory of evolution?

427. If you woke up with a huge cold sore on your lip the day of your senior pictures?

428. If you accidentally started a forest fire?

429. If your dog chewed up your prized collection of rare and expensive collectibles?

430. If you could be any character in "Star Wars"?

431. If William Hung of "American Idol" fame showed up to sing at your wedding?

432. If you found an original Leonardo DaVinci painting in your attic?

433. If you saw something that was stolen from you listed on eBay?

434. If someone was talking on her cell phone behind you during a movie?

435. If you were in a restaurant and someone at the next table started choking?

436. If you put a bucket of water on top of a door with the intention of it dumping on your friend when he walked in, but his mom opened the door instead?

437. If, as you walked into a restaurant where you were going to propose to your girl-friend, you accidentally dropped the engagement ring down a sewer drain?

438. If you saw someone drowning at the beach but there was no lifeguard?

439. If you were carrying a cake into the room for your child's birthday while everyone was singing "Happy Birthday" and you dropped the cake on the floor right in front of her?

440. If the person sitting next to you on the plane started telling you about all of her problems?

441. If you were watching a movie at your friend's house, his dad walked in, kicked off his shoes, and his feet stunk up the whole room?

442. If as you walked out on the ice to sing the national anthem at a hockey game you slipped and fell?

443. If there was a brown paper bag on fire on your porch?

444. If you woke up with a spider egg in your ear?

445. If there was no more ESPN?

446. If you had no heat or air conditioning?

447. If you gave someone a gift but forgot to take the price tag off?

448. If your sister wanted a pet pig?

449. If you went to someone's house and they had a "no shoes" rule—and your feet reeked?

450. If you were sitting in a restaurant and your chair broke?

451. If you could ask God one question?

452. If you were asked to come up with one solution for ending world poverty?

453. If your parents left you in charge of the house for a week while they went away?

454. If the person sitting next to you on the plane fell asleep and leaned his head on your shoulder and began to drool on you?

455. If your pants ripped while doing a drama in front of your church?

456. If no church buildings existed?

457. If you knew for certain that you would live to be one hundred years old?

458. If someone laughed so hard that a booger flew out of his nose and onto you?

459. If you could choose any point in history in which to live?

460. If you showed up at a theme park and it was closed?

461. If your friend said that all religions lead to heaven?

462. If your parents disapproved of the person you wanted to marry?

463. If you could spend the day with Jesus' twelve disciples?

464. If you could change one thing about your school?

465. If your parents read your personal journal?

466. If you had no legs?

467. If you were put in a room with no windows and forced to listen to opera for one week straight?

468. If you could become any animal?

469. If the Lord revealed to you that a reaction you had during a recent argument with someone did not line up with Scripture or His heart in the situation?

470. If you caught a home run ball by the opposing team at Wriggly Field?

471. If Michael Jordan was your dad?

472. If you were stranded on an island?

473. If you were stuck in traffic on a large bridge after eating two bran muffins and drinking a really strong cup of coffee?

474. If your brother or sister borrowed your favorite CD and lost it?

475. If you were changing in the bathroom on the plane, lost your balance, and when you leaned on the door it opened and you fell out into the aisle?

476. If you lost all of your toes and fingers to frostbite while mountain climbing?

477. If Donald Trump asked you to design a hotel for him inside and out?

478. If your mom or dad had Alzheimer's?

479. If your parents told you during your senior year of high school that your mom was pregnant?

480. If you were swimming in a public pool and saw something brown floating in the water?

481. If you had to go to summer school?

482. If you were in Mexico and they served you tacos with extremely hot salsa?

483. If you could improve a skill that you have?

484. If you were told you would be single for your entire life?

485. If someone with really bad breath was talking with you?

486. If you were asked to identify the number one problem facing your generation?

487. If you had to live with inexplicable pain for the rest of your life?

488. If you had to devise a strategy for winning "Survivor"?

489. If your family was stuck in the house together for an entire week due to a massive snowstorm?

490. If you got separated from your group while in New York City?

491. If you could tell "Pimp My Ride" how to pimp out your car?

492. If you could spend the day with the Apostle Paul?

493. If you could write an eleventh commandment?

494. If it rained all day, every day of your beach vacation?

495. If you found out you could not have biological children?

496. If you could change one thing about computers?

497. If you were swimming in the ocean and felt something bump your foot?

498. If you could rap freestyle about the good things you see in the person to your right?

499. If you could dispel one misconception that unchurched people have about church?

500. If you could come up with some ***What Would You Do?*** questions that aren't in this book? If you have some good ones, or your group comes up with some, e-mail them to <u>wwydquestion@yahoo.com</u>. You can also post comments about how the questions have worked in your group at <u>www.myspace/wwydquestion</u>. Drop by and share your stories with us!

Endnotes

1. Schulenburg, Brian *Choose Your Top 3* (El Cajon: Zondervan/Youth Specialties, 2006).
2. http://movies.about.com/od/napoleondyna-mite/a/dynamite051505.htm